DAISY A DAY

Hope for a Grieving Heart

HARRIET HODGSON

North Carolina

Published in the United States by WriteLife Publishing, Inc.
(an imprint of Boutique of Quality Books Publishing Company, Inc.)
www.writelife.com

978-1-60808-270-4 (p)
978-1-60808-271-1 (e)

Library of Congress Control Number: 2022933240

Book design by Robin Krauss, www.bookformatters.com
Cover design by Rebecca Lown, www.rebeccalowndesign.com
Cover photo from www.istockphotos.com
Editor: Andrea Vande Vorde

PRAISE FOR
DAISY A DAY
AND HARRIET HODGSON

"Filled with hope and encouragement, Harriet Hodgson's guide for mourners is a handbook of survival, offering practical tips and useful tools for getting through each day while navigating the many challenges of grief. Based on her experience of coping with her own significant losses, she includes lessons learned from each—all presented in her characteristic style: simple, understandable, easy to digest, filled with hope and encouragement, and grounded in valid and reliable research. Highly recommended."

– Marty Tousley, RN, MS, FT, Grief Counselor and author of *Finding Your Way Through Grief: A Guide for the First Year*

"This is the best grief book I have ever read. Harriet Hodgson's extraordinary losses give her an unrivaled expertise. She uses this to help all of us when we are faced with loss. Her healing behaviors and suggestions go beyond the usual. We all need to keep this book handy for ourselves and as a gift to others. Loss is universal."

- Mary Amundsen, RN, BSN, MS in Counseling

"*Daisy A Day* is more than a book. It's a friend. It will climb onto the couch with you and hand you a warm cup of comfort tea. It's a book to carry with you, to open at any page, to digest in short, friendly spurts. The suggestions, ideas, and insights come from years of loving experience brought together by Harriet's creativity and empathy. It's a book for new grievers and for those of us who have been on the journey for a while. Sit back, invite it to join you, and feel comforted and loved."

– Joy Brown, founder of Centering Corporation, author of about 50 books, and author of *The BOOB Girls* comedy mystery series for senior women

"A daisy appears as a simple flower representing innocence and purity, yet its symbolism is far more complicated. And, in truth, the daisy is two flowers in one: the petals and cluster of disc petals. So too is this book. At once serious and cheeky. In *Daisy A Day*, Hodgson creates an incredible book, a masterful, poetic how-to that escorts us, like a beloved friend, through the ordinary sacredness of grief."

– Elizabeth Coplan, Grief Dialogues Found and Chief Playwright

"At the bedside, we palliative and hospice doctors can offer plenty of medication, but the one prescription I like to write is that for hope. We always have hope. And when a loved one has left you, we are left with hope for an end to the grief we feel. Harriet Hodgson helps us get there, one daisy at a time. I am honored to know her."

– Edward T. Creagan, MDE, FAAHPM, Emeritus Professor of Medical Oncology, Mayo Clinic Medical School, author of *Farewell: Vital End-of-Life Questions with Candid Answers from a Leading Palliative and Hospice Physician*

"The title, *Daisy A Day*, at first seems to defy the subject matter of Harriet Hodgson's latest book; this one on grief, but it is exactly that contrast that makes it such a valuable class in coaching.

Reading it, as a member of the choir, I found her guidance spot on. The short life lessons are just what someone finding themselves in onset, middle, and latter part of the grieving journey will find sweetly digestible. Broken up into stages of grief, you can open any page within a section and find words of encouragement, wisdom, experience and examples in bite-size pieces . . . about the attention span of someone in the early stages of grief . . . a sentence or two.

At The Caregiver Space, we encounter many issues having to do with the practical side of after caregiving: the aspects of loneliness, feeling lost, fearful, forgotten by friends and, of course, overwhelmed. Harriet's new book will be at the top of my list for both new mourners and those who are sadly stuck in a vicious cycle they see no way out of. Harriet holds your hand, showing you many different ways you can help yourself and see the future."

– Adrienne Gruberg, Founder and President,
The Caregiver Space, Inc.

"Harriet Hodgson's *Daisy A Day: Hope for a Grieving Heart* captures pearls of raw grief experiences and transforms the pain of grief into healing principles. Her delightful style and wisdom, built on a career of working with grief, transpose daily thoughts into a road map for thriving with small healing steps. (#128).

I wish I had the benefit of her book earlier in my grief journey."

– Stedman Stevens, author of *A Beautiful Life: The Little Things That Help Grieving Families*

"Beginning with some of the largest and universal questions about grief and loss, Harriet Hodgson avoids the temptation to search for easy answers. Instead, she invites readers to find simple practices to accompany their grief in a way that only someone who has lived with grief can do. *Daisy A Day* is deeply honest and lovingly practical, making it both a delight to read and a book that can make a difference is someone's daily life."

– Reverend Luke Stevens-Royer

"Harriet Hodgson's personal experiences with losing loved ones has equipped her with an abundance of wisdom which shines through in *Daisy A Day*. Filled with comfort, understanding, and useful tips, this book is a true gift for anyone facing loss."

– Lynda Cheldelin Fell, founding partner,
International Grief Institute

This book is for all who grieve.
Grief links us together and we will
survive it together.

CONTENTS

OPENING THOUGHTS

Grief is part of the human condition. We all go through it, yet when it finds us, life seems unfair. We are devastated and angry. Why did my loved one die now? What will happen to me? Will I ever be happy again? These questions rattle around in our minds. So many thoughts go through our minds we can hardly think. Two minutes after we read an article, we forget it. We walk into a room and wonder why we are there.

Life becomes scary. Some of our feelings are scary too.

I wrote *Daisy A Day* to understand grief feelings. Grief and I are well acquainted. I am a bereaved wife, mother, daughter, sister, daughter-in-law, cousin, and friend. Four months after my husband died, I started writing this book. I usually have an inkling of what my next book will be. Not this time. *Daisy A Day* was a surprise, an idea that came to me at four o'clock in the morning.

Evidently my subconscious mind had been taking notes for years. These thoughts accumulated and bubbled until they burst forth like a geyser. After four family members died in a row—my daughter (mother of my twin grandchildren), father-in-law, brother, and the twins' father—I made a promise to myself. *Grief will be the loser; life will be the winner.* I would make it so.

Grief feelings, ways of coping, challenges, problems, and solutions are described in *Daisy A Day*. I liked the symbolism of the daisy, a sweet white flower with a happy yellow center, so I used it in the title. Some think daisies symbolize innocence. You may have been innocent about the complexities of grief until you experienced it. Grief comes at different times and in different forms.

You are probably familiar with the idea of pulling petals off a daisy and saying, *He loves me, he loves me not* or, *she loves me, she loves me not.* Well, you don't have to worry about love, for it is stronger than death. Love and grief are joined together. If you didn't love your husband, wife, partner, sibling, child, relative, or pet, you wouldn't grieve.

Grief is proof of love.

But American society doesn't understand our feelings. Grief is the elephant in the room and we are part of the herd. Society sends us an unspoken message: *Don't talk about grief.* The message is sent with facial expressions, body language, attitude, and comments like, "You are a strong person." Some say this to be encouraging. Others use the sentence as a dismissal; the conversation is over.

I heard "You are a strong person" so many times I wanted to scream. This became a dreaded sentence. Yes, I am a strong person, but strong people get weary and falter. You may be faltering now. We stumble and get up again because that is our only choice. I continue to write because it is what I do. Writing is more than my occupation; it is my passion.

Daisy A Day is my story—and yours—a story of pain and survival.

Unfortunately, life doesn't stop and wait for us. We still need to care for kids, grocery shop, fix meals, clean the house, do laundry, and pay bills. A week after my daughter died, I went to the grocery store. As I pushed my cart along the aisles, I spotted a friend of mine. My friend saw me, gasped in surprise, turned her cart around, and sped away. Wasn't I worth a "Hello," or "I'm so sorry," or "How are you doing?" Apparently not.

I felt hurt and sick.

Since then, more family members have died, and I learned something from each loss. Grief has made me a stronger, more empathetic person. Every now and then, however, I need a boost, words of encouragement to keep me going. You may need a boost and *Daisy A*

Day is that boost, a friend you may turn to again and again. It is divided into sections that match your grief journey.

- Shock and Anguish
- Coping and Finding Balance
- A New and Meaningful Life
- Making Good from Grief

Since you don't need a tome, I have kept the readings short and simple, nuggets of information to get you through the day. The words come from years of grief research. You may start reading anywhere and stop reading anywhere. Our grief experiences are similar. Because of death, we treasure every second of life. Because of sorrow, we understand the light of joy. Because people gave to us, we give to others.

We give ourselves a verbal daisy a day and smile.

SHOCK AND ANGUISH

(1)

You are in the dark depths of grief, down so deep you do not want to get out of bed. Getting up and getting dressed are the first healing steps. Take them.

(2)

Tears express feelings. Make a conscious decision to cry anywhere, anytime, for as long as you need. Crying can lead to some odd experiences. (I cried in the grocery store next to tomatoes and olive oil.) Let yourself cry.

(3)

The death of a child is an out-of-turn death—nature's mistake. You are shattered because you have been robbed of the present and the future. The realization is agonizing. Be grateful for the time you had with your child.

(4)

Grief can make you an unsafe driver. Use a buddy system to prevent accidents. Appoint one person as the driver and another as a lookout. Swap roles every time you get in the car. The buddy system works. Keep using it.

(5)

Just thinking about food makes you nauseous. You need food so you eat an egg and a bite of toast for dinner. Fruit would have been nice, but an egg is all you can manage. That is okay. A little food is better than none.

(6)

In some cultures, people wear white armbands to show they are grieving. Wear an armband if you think it would be helpful. Be prepared to answer the question, "Who are you mourning?"

(7)

The sympathy cards keep coming. Reading them is so painful you stop reading. Stash the cards in a box or basket. Read them when you feel stronger. Sympathy cards say things people cannot.

(8)

Television news is on twenty-four hours a day. Keeping up with the news is one thing, feeling devastated by it is another. Watch the morning news and do not watch any more. The news will come around again. And again. And again.

(9)

Grief leads to negative thoughts. Every time a negative thought comes to mind, balance it with a positive one. This takes practice, but you can do it. Regulate your negative thoughts.

(10)

Avoid depressed people (You know who they are). Connect with upbeat people (You know who they are). This decision turns dark days into brighter ones. Thank goodness for friends!

(11)

Friends think saying your deceased loved one's name will make you sad. The opposite is true. You need to say their name and say it often. If you are the only one who hears the name, that is enough.

(12)

Shock affects your body. You may have a dry throat, nausea, diarrhea, heart palpitations, headaches, back pain, and more. Some bereaved people obsess about their health. Avoid this path because it leads you in circles.

(13)

The intense pain of grief can lead to *grief heart*—high blood pressure and the symptoms of a heart attack. If you have symptoms of a heart attack, see a doctor immediately. You need to know if you have developed grief heart.

(14)

When you awaken in the morning, think of friends who have helped you. You would not be where you are today without their help. Friends are supportive and help ease the shock of grief.

(15)

Your sense of humor is dormant now. Remember your humor and keep it handy. (After our daughter died, I told my husband my wacky New York sense of humor would save me. It did.) Give yourself permission to laugh. Small as it is, a chuckle can save the day.

(16)

Make a list of the organizations to notify about your loved one's death. This list should include names, contact dates, and discussion points—documentation that saves you hassles in the future.

(17)

Well-meaning people give you terrible advice. There is no substitute for grief experience. Seek advice from those who have walked the walk and talked the talk. Ignore poor advice.

(18)

Writing your loved one's obituary is so painful you barely get a word on paper. You are overcome with tears. Take a break. Work on the obituary in stages until it is finished.

(19)

If you are asked to pick a word that describes you, *broken* is the word. Your soul is broken. Glue it back together with patience, learning, and self-care. Though you may have a tiny crack in your soul, you no longer feel broken.

(20)

Will you cry forever? The answer is "no." Hard as it is to believe, the day will come when you cry less, and sense a change in grief. Life is starting to look brighter.

(21)

Independence is one of your traits. While this is admirable, now is not the time to be super-independent. Ask family members for help. One helpful gesture can be a lifesaver.

(22)

You had one crisis and could have another. Prepare for them. Enter emergency numbers into your smartphone or stick a printed list by your landline phone. Good for you.

(23)

Many people do not know what to say to someone who is grieving. You hear strange—even hurtful—comments. Responding to these comments is a waste of time. Thank these people and go on your way.

(24)

So many feelings. So much pain. Divide your feelings into two categories—awful and awe-full. Regret is awful. Being alive is awe-full. Hold awe-full ideas close to your heart.

(25)

Shock slows you down so much you feel like a sloth. You cannot seem to get moving. Sloth times are thinking times and you need them. Do not feel badly about being a sloth.

(26)

Grief affects relationships. People you thought would help do not. People you barely know step forward to help. It is so confusing. The best person to help is you, a reliable, loving, caring person.

(27)

You still cannot believe your loved one died. Are you asleep or awake? Acceptance is a journey of its own. Keep telling yourself the news is true. Sooner or later, you will come to believe it.

(28)

Brace yourself. The support you received a few weeks ago will fade. No more calls. No more flowers. No more casseroles. Friends seem to have fallen off the earth. Be your own friend and be strong.

(29)

Relatives want to help, so they start clearing out kitchen drawers, cupboards, and even the garage. Their timing is terrible. You are not ready for these things. Ask relatives to please stop what they are doing. Be firm.

(30)

Grief brain is a combination of confusion and forget-fulness. You may do surprising things. (I lost an egg, another story for another time.) Watch for symptoms of grief brain. Postpone major decisions until your brain is back on track.

(31)

Are you struggling with anger? Express this feeling by walloping a pillow or pounding a punching bag. Discharging anger is calming and allows you to get on with healing.

(32)

Some turn to alcohol to dull their shock and anguish. Alcohol can dull feelings, but excessive drinking prolongs them. You do not want to grieve forever. Be smart. Monitor consumption if you use alcohol.

(33)

Mundane tasks—making the bed, folding the laundry, and drying dishes—are comforting. Doing these tasks proves you are still functioning. Grief has not taken over your life. This is good news.

(34)

Diversion works. Watch inspiring or entertaining television programs. One channel excels at this. Watch regularly, and you will recognize the actors, the plots, and even the props. All the movies end happily.

(35)

Grief support is available online. Before you join a group, answer these questions: Who owns the website? Who writes for it? Does the website push products? Leave if you are unable to find the answers. You do not need to be duped *and* grieving.

(36)

You want to push back at grief and keep pushing. This may be a good time to ease off a bit. Push occasionally and let your body accommodate to the death of your loved one. You will survive grief.

(37)

According to folklore, music soothes the savage beast. Grief is your savage beast. Calm it by listening to soothing music. You may choose to keep music on all day for company.

(38)

Items that connect you with your loved one are called *linking objects*. Using these objects is comforting. Wearing them is more comforting. You may wear your loved one's ring, one of the best linking objects ever.

(39)

Your grief is as unique as your thumbprint. Do not worry about how others grieve. Instead, grieve in your own way and in your own time. Hold yourself together for one more day.

(40)

Grief has its good days, bad days, and in-between days. When you get up in the morning you do not know which kind of day you will have. A day is a day. Just do the best you can.

(41)

Ask widows, widowers, and bereaved parents how they coped with the shock of death. A widow may pretend her husband is in the next room and talk to him daily. Try this if you think it might help.

(42)

You and your loved one used to eat together. Now the thought of eating at the table by yourself is so painful you eat standing up. You are not the first person to do this. We all have our grief quirks.

(43)

Stress continues to build. Try diaphragmatic breathing to calm yourself. When you breathe from your diaphragm, your heart rate slows, and your blood pressure drops. Better yet, you can do this type of breathing anywhere.

(44)

Lack of sympathy cards does not mean friends are uncaring. It means friends have not heard your sad news and are busy with their lives. You do not need to overthink sympathy cards.

(45)

Your shock is so great you forget to drink enough liquids and get dehydrated. Water is the best thirst quencher. (My mother called water Adam's Ale.) Raise a glass of Adam's Ale to your loved one and yourself.

(46)

How many death certificates do you need? Some organizations accept photocopied death certificates, and some do not. Be prepared. Order ten certificates in case you need them.

(47)

Legal notices keep arriving. Read them carefully and read them again. Resist the urge to pile these documents on the kitchen counter. File legal documents in a home file or safe deposit box.

(48)

The bed for two is now a bed for one—you. There is no one to cuddle, no one to hold onto after a bad dream, no one to warm you on a chilly night. Move to your loved one's side of the bed. Snuggle in and think of them.

(49)

Shock generates more questions than answers. Be gentle with yourself. You do not need to answer all your questions now. Later, when your shock is less, you may pursue answers.

(50)

Grief is stranger than you imagined. How can you help yourself? Start meditating. Learn about different types of meditation and try one. Daily meditation helps calm a wounded soul.

(51)

Watch for additional signs of grief brain: clerical errors, unpaid bills, confusing the facts, poor decisions, and odd experiences (I put a comb in the refrigerator). Ask a relative to watch for signs of grief brain.

(52)

Exercise is a way of coping. Walking is the easiest form of exercise. Walk outside when it is sunny. Walk inside at a mall when it is rainy. A fifteen-minute walk can change your outlook on life.

(53)

Asking for help is an act of courage. Be specific with these requests. "Will you make the arrangements?" "I would love to ride with you." A little help can lower stress markedly.

(54)

Maybe you asked God to give you strength as your loved one was dying. You received the strength you needed. More painful days are ahead. Pray for your loved one and yourself.

(55)

Making a timeline helps you understand your grief history. Draw a horizontal line across paper. Write the names of deceased loved ones above the line. Write dates of their deaths below the line. (You can guess.) Now you see the scope of your grief.

(56)

Early humans probably felt the same feelings you are feeling now. They felt the same shock and anguish when loved ones died. Grief ties you to the past, present, and future. Humankind is with you.

(57)

The thought of fixing a meal is daunting. Make a big batch of Whatever Soup. Combine whatever vegetables you have with chicken, beef, or vegetable stock. Enjoy soup for lunch or dinner. Freeze the rest for another day.

(58)

"How many children do you have?" is a jarring question for bereaved parents. Prepare answers to it. One answer: "I have a surviving daughter (or son)." This states a fact and reflects your grief history.

(59)

You worry constantly. Keeping a worry box may be helpful. When you have a worry, jot it down on a small piece of paper and put the paper in a box. A few weeks later read your worries. Many may have disappeared.

(60)

You wish grief came with a warning tag: CAUTION: PITFALLS AHEAD. Be on the lookout for more anguish, unrealistic expectations, and family squabbles. Avoid these pitfalls.

(61)

Truth is stranger than fiction. Months after your loved one dies, another loved one may die. Shock and anguish return and your brain is traumatized. Grief is a sacred experience and remembering this helps.

(62)

People tell you sad stories. You have sad stories of your own and do not need more. End the conversation as best you can. (I look at my watch and say I am late for a doctor's appointment.) Thank the person for their concern and leave.

(63)

Just when you were feeling better, grief grabs you by the throat. You feel like your loved one died yesterday. There will always be yesterdays in your life. Prepare for them.

(64)

Did your loved one just say "Hon?" The voice you hear is in your mind. When this happens, recall the loving things your beloved said. Let these words wrap their arms around you.

(65)

"How are you?" is a question people often ask. You say "fine" when you are not. Pretending you are fine is exhausting. Instead of "fine," say "okay," "getting along," or "making progress."

(66)

Talking about painful truths, like scattering your loved one's ashes, makes these truths bearable. Bring up painful topics when you are with family members. Share feelings and discuss solutions.

(67)

You do not ask for pity. All you want is understanding. Some understand your shock and others do not. Stick with the understanding folks because they will probably stick with you.

(68)

Before your loved one died, you did not see the big picture of their life. Now you see it clearly. Your loved one made the world a better place. Let this thought inspire you.

(69)

Your loved one may have had one-liners like "Don't burn your bridges." These sayings are part of your conversation. Add another saying to your list: *I will survive grief.* Make this your promise, your mission, your goal.

(70)

You would not be where you are today without the help of others. Help them in return. Call a grieving friend and compare your responses to grief. Each of you may help the other.

(71)

Grief experts recommend journaling to cope with grief. Buy a blank book and start your journal. Write about your experiences, feelings, and problems. Some journal entries may surprise you, and that is okay. You are a surprising person.

(72)

Do not worry if a friend's grief differs from yours. Just do your grief work. This includes things you *must* do and things you *want* to do. Cross off the tasks one by one. You are making progress.

(73)

Special days trigger grief. You may burst into tears on your loved one's birthday or on your wedding anniversary. Prepare for these days. Plan an activity, hang out with friends, or take a mini trip. This diversion helps you get through the day.

(74)

Days pass by like a blur. You are still in shock and still have grief brain. Recovering from grief brain is a slow, gradual process. Six months from now, though you have occasional bouts of grief brain, you will be able to tell your brain is better.

(75)

You try to avoid tasks associated with your loved one's death. Sometimes it is better to tackle tasks immediately. Put credit cards in your name if you had joint accounts. This makes things easier for you.

(76)

Fix a meal that includes some of your loved one's favorite foods—hamburgers, cookies, or (gasp) hot peppers. Remember the feelings you had when you and your loved one ate together. Here's to you, dear one.

(77)

Your "To Do" list is a "Not Done" list. Tasks that your loved one used to do are piling up. Grit your teeth, pick a task, and do it. Accomplishing one task gives you the courage to tackle others. Hurray for you!

(78)

You take prescribed medications. Before, your loved one reminded you to take them. Now you are the reminder person. Be safe. Keep a log of the medicine you take and the dosages.

(79)

Your laugh may be as rusty as an old hinge, but it is still a laugh, and you need that. Watch television or online comedies. Laughter really is good medicine.

(80)

Sweatshirts have slogans on them. One says *Inhale Courage, Exhale Fear*, a good slogan. When you inhale, you take in life-giving oxygen. When you exhale, you rid your body of carbon dioxide. Let go of fear with every breath you release.

(81)

People express sympathy in different ways. Try to focus on the intent of the expression, even though the expression itself can feel uncomfortable.

(82)

Visualization helps to calm anxiety. Close your eyes and imagine you are sitting on a sandy beach. You watch the foamy waves, hear squawking seagulls, and feel the warmth of the sun. Every time you have a terrible thought, dismiss it from your mind.

(83)

Talk openly about your grief. The more you share your thoughts, the more bearable they become. Experienced mourners may have had the same thoughts you are having. You are not crazy; you are normal.

(84)

Your feelings bounce around like a rubber ball. One day you are upbeat. The next day you wallow in grief. Grief mood swings are part of grief. As time passes, your moods will even out. Be patient with yourself.

(85)

File burial or cremation arrangements in a manila folder. Add legal documents and receipts to this file. You hate doing this and must do this. That is the reality of death. You are caring for your loved one until the very end.

(86)

Calm yourself with stretching. Stand and stretch your arms and legs. Shake your limbs too. Spending a few minutes on stretching helps you shake off grief.

(87)

You feel hollow inside. Getting back to yourself requires patience. Resist the urge to race through grief. Proceed slowly and take all the time you need. Observe life and yourself.

(88)

When it comes to grief healing, do the best you can with the time you have. You will make good progress some days and less progress other days. Still, you are making progress. Give a cheer.

(89)

Laughter is good for your health. Treasure the laughs you shared with your loved one. If you listen carefully, you may hear their laughter and even laugh yourself. Laughter is a sign of progress.

(90)

You thought you understood grief until you experienced it. Read grief healing books to understand the scope of grief. Pay attention to the symptoms. Put a checkmark by the ones you have.

(91)

You have heard so many "you should" comments you want to scream. Strangers even give you advice. Seek advice from experienced grievers. Learn from their experience.

(92)

Friends send you flowers. All the flowers are lovely, but one bouquet may stand out from the rest. For me it was all white—lilies, daisies, roses, and flowers I could not identify. White is a symbol of hope. Was there a certain flower or flower color that lifted you up?

(93)

Even though those around you might not understand, talking about and remembering your loved one can help you heal. Find people who will let you do that.

COPING AND FINDING BALANCE

(94)

Elisabeth Kübler-Ross created stages of grief—denial, anger, bargaining, depression, acceptance—as guidelines. Since Kubler-Ross came up with these stages, grief experts have added more. Pay attention to stages that seem the most logical to you.

(95)

Though you cannot change facts, you can alter your responses to them. You have the power to write a good ending to your story. Use this power. Consider several endings. Which would be best?

(96)

Eating is still a problem. Ease back into eating slowly. Have a small amount of food. A few hours later, eat some more. Repeat this pattern. Your body needs fuel, and you are eating.

(97)

Smiling is good for your health. When you smile your brain releases endorphins—chemicals that prompt happy feelings. Though you want to smile, you cannot. Practice smiling in front of a mirror. Your smile will once again be natural someday.

(98)

The first laugh after a loved one dies surprises you. This laugh is a milestone and proves you are healing. Circle this day on the calendar. Draw a smiley face too. Maybe life will turn out all right after all.

(99)

Remember your loved one's personality. How did their personality affect you? Think of all the times your loved one helped you. Thank goodness for your loved one's strength.

(100)

Church memorial services have become virtual online services. Plan your loved one's virtual service. Honor their life with photos, readings, memories, and music. Make the service as memorable as your loved one.

(101)

Grief feelings change in an instant. Name a feeling—scared, lost, angry, confused, etc.—the minute you feel it. At the end of the day, consider the range of emotions you felt. These feelings link you with others who are grieving.

(102)

Grief myths abound. The myth, "Time heals all wounds," is partially true. Time eases your grief but does not erase it. Grief will always be part of your life. Do not be diverted by grief myths.

(103)

"Will I survive?" you ask. Counter this question with a pledge: *I will get through this.* Make this pledge your mantra. Say it every day. Believe it with all your heart.

(104)

The Compassionate Friends is an organization for bereaved parents and families. Each December, TCF has an international candle lighting. Learn more about it and participate. As you light your candle, envision thousands of candles being lit around the globe. You are not alone.

(105)

Read excerpts from your journal. Are your thoughts the same or have they changed? Look for grief stages and identify problems and possible solutions. Keeping a journal is bargain therapy, one of the best things you can do for yourself.

(106)

Flowering plants lift your spirits. Have at least one flowering plant in your home. Watching flowers bud and bloom is fun. The tiny flowers give you hope. Tend to hope as carefully as you tend flowers.

(107)

Ask an adult child or other relative to call you each day. Regular calls benefit both of you. You may find you and your adult child have more in common than you realized. Then, too, it is good to hear their voice.

(108)

You are still here—a survivor—and feel guilty about it. Survivor's guilt is a non-productive emotion. Cast this guilt aside. Your loved one is part of you and always will be. Now you are the keeper of dreams.

(109)

Grief is all you think about, especially if several loved ones died in a row. Recovering from multiple losses takes longer than recovering from one. More than any other time, this is a time to be gentle with yourself.

(110)

Like the illuminated sign in Times Square, self-talk keeps going through your mind. Flash, flash, flash. These messages come from your subconscious and conscious mind. Pay attention to the messages. Some news flashes may surprise you.

(111)

Silence enables you to hear your soul. Enjoy at least a half hour of silence a day. Listen long and listen hard. Consider each idea. One idea may determine your future.

(112)

Think of a funny time you shared with your loved one. (The airline lost our luggage on the way to Yugoslavia. I washed the clothes we were wearing. When the concierge called to say the tour was leaving, I blurted, "Our clothes are wet and we are naked." The silence was deafening.) Memories like this will always be funny. Find strength in them.

(113)

Anticipatory grief can shorten post-death grief, according to some experts. Before your loved one died, anticipatory grief followed you around like a black storm cloud. You survived the storm. Build on this experience.

(114)

You do not have to be friends with everyone in a support group to benefit from meetings. Sample a few meetings. Listen attentively to what is said. One idea can be a game-changer for you.

(115)

What was your loved one's favorite hymn or song? Sing it at the top of your lungs. The song is a tribute to your loved one. Hum it as you bustle about. Make their song your song of life.

(116)

Do not let angry feelings fester. Set your sights on forgiveness and let go of anger. Forgiveness is a powerful feeling, maybe even more powerful than anger. You are a forgiving person.

(117)

Write another letter to your loved one. How does it differ from the first letter? When you feel like it, write more letters. Be honest with your feelings. Save your letters because they may be helpful someday.

(118)

Religion is comforting but it does not immunize you from grief. You still grieve. Members of your religious community are anxious to help you, so let them. In the process, they get to know you and you get to know them.

(119)

Jobs still need to get done. Some jobs are so threatening you cannot start them. Use the divide-and-conquer approach. Divide your big job into smaller parts and work on each one. Nicely done!

(120)

Anger creates energy. Put this energy to good use. Apply it to personal, household, and community tasks. Use the energy of anger to improve your life. Keep generating positive energy.

(121)

Mental chatter can get out of hand. If you obsess about the past, you miss the present. That is bad news. The good news is that you can control chatter. Brighten your day with positive thoughts.

(122)

Maybe your loved one made you a better person. You may have made them a better person too. Though your loved one is gone, you feel their love and always will. What a blessing.

(123)

Your mind is a storehouse of memories. They awaken you in the middle of the night and come back at odd times of the day. Leave sad memories in the past where they belong. Savor happy memories.

(124)

Ugh. You have so much unfinished grief business you feel crazy. Choose one task and start working on it. Keep working until the task is done. Finish unfinished business before it finishes you.

(125)

"Broken heart" is an apt description of your grief. Repairing your heart takes introspection and time. Look inside yourself. Your heart is broken, yet your spirit is intact. Tap that spirit today.

(126)

Many people (even those who do not like it) read poetry after a loved one dies. You may be one of them. Poetic words make you think about life. Your life is a poem, with a beginning, an end, and a cadence of its own.

(127)

Read about Near-Death Experiences (NDE) by those who have experienced them. These stories will make you wonder and may comfort you. Still, as it has for centuries, death will remain a mystery.

(128)

Grief healing is measured in inches. You make your way slowly and hope you are headed in the right direction. Inches become feet, feet become yards, and yards become miles. You are making progress and have come a long way.

(129)

Though you are feeling down and lack motivation, get up and dance around. Doing the opposite of what you are thinking can recharge you. Besides, you have some mighty good moves.

(130)

The idea that grief generates anger is common. You are the exception. Despite the common belief, you are not angry at God or life or your loved one. However, you may get angry at the things people say. Put this anger to good use.

(131)

Grief teaches you to be direct with condolences. No struggling for words. No platitudes. When you meet a bereaved person, you get to the point: "I am sorry _____ died." That is all they need to hear.

(132)

You have met bereaved people who are happy. They are always smiling. How do they do it? Hang out with these people. Bask in their spirit. Learn how they created happiness for themselves.

(133)

Videos of your loved one's final days keep playing in your mind. Stop them. Picture a happy scenario instead—the people, the colors, the setting, and the conversation. Play this mental video often.

(134)

Grief is a tug of war. Your feelings are tugged one way and then the other. Recognize opposite feelings and let yourself feel them. Developing this awareness is another grief journey.

(135)

Relatives invite you for dinner. Grandkids come and visit. Friends send you cards. Despite loving gestures, you still feel alone. You are not alone; you are supported by past and future generations of family.

(136)

Count your blessings—whatever they may be. You have family and friends. Love is the biggest blessing of all. Be glad that you were loved.

(137)

Some believe God does not give us more than we can handle. Not you. You know many people who have too much to handle. Ignore this saying if it makes you uncomfortable. Just keep doing your grief work.

(138)

Find a photo of your loved one and have it made into a puzzle. As you fit the pieces together, think of how your life and your loved one's life fit together. Each of you was the other one's missing piece.

(139)

Words are powerful. Delete corrosive and upsetting words from your mind. Replace them with positive words. Start with *love, grateful, kind, understand, know,* and *happy.* Continue to add positive words to your list.

(140)

Look for beauty today. A dandelion blooming in a sidewalk crack can be as beautiful as a rose. Shadows on the same sidewalk have intriguing shapes. Find hidden beauty wherever you can.

(141)

Months have passed. You feel as badly now as when you first heard the tragic news. This may be the time to meet with a certified grief counselor. A few sessions can get you moving forward again.

(142)

Grieving children, even kids six to eight years old, can become depressed. If your child is anxious and has behavior problems, they may be in the early stages of depression. Make an appointment with a pediatrician ASAP.

(143)

Earl A. Grollman wrote many books about grief and is often quoted. This quote may comfort you: "The only cure for grief is to grieve." Think about Grollman's quote and follow his advice.

(144)

Start a visual journal of grief. Buy a sketchbook. Express your feelings with doodles. When your sketchbook is full, buy another and keep doodling. Doodle your way through grief.

(145)

You know them—the people who moan and exaggerate constantly. Their behavior wears you out. Avoid the drama folks. Life is dramatic enough and you do not need more drama.

(146)

The numbness of grief abates slowly. If you continue your grief work, numbness gives way to awareness and a renewed interest in life. Watch for signs of this awareness.

(147)

You are sick of grief. Enough already. This is not the time to give up. Talk to others who are grieving. Which coping steps work for them? Believe in yourself and keep going.

(148)

Something wonderful just happened. You turn to share the joyful news with your loved one and they are not there. What a disappointment. Life's lesson: To feel joy fully, it needs to be shared.

(149)

Grief is the most painful experience of life. You want to avoid pain and, no matter what you do, cannot escape it. In time, grief gives way to hope. Keep the candle of hope burning.

(150)

Memory is a gift. You remember sad moments, happy ones, and life-changing ones. Use memories to remember and solidify your identity. You are a memorable person.

(151)

Life and death are intertwined. Grief is an inescapable journey. Everyone who lives will die, even you. Be grateful for this day and live it joyfully.

(152)

Since your grief journey is yours alone, others do not see it clearly. Some observers may think you are overreacting. Really? Try to ignore these comments. Stay on your healing path and keep walking forward.

(153)

Fear weighs you down. You have the power to face fear and release it. Of course, you cannot release all fears, but releasing some lightens the load you are carrying. What a relief.

(154)

Life is sacred. Watch for sacred moments in the day: a baby's cry, a robin's song, an orange sunset. Sacred moments abound and ease your grief journey. Pray for all life, including yours.

(155)

Bask in the warmth of the sun. Sit by a sunny window or outdoors. While you are sitting there, imagine the universe, our world, and our sun. You came from stars and will return to them.

(156)

Feeling close to nature is soothing. Make outdoor activity part of each day. Go for a walk, sit on a park bench, or putter in the garden. A few minutes outside can boost your mood.

(157)

A month can seem like a year when you are grieving. Think of the time you shared with your loved one. Remember your feelings and let them heal your grieving heart.

(158)

Grief is tough, demanding, and complex. Fight it like a warrior. You have the strength and have been amassing it all your life, month by month and year by year. There is a wellspring of strength inside you.

159)

Get up early and watch the sunrise. Witness the changing colors and the shifting rays. See the light-dappled treetops, buildings, your home, and your face. Hello, sun. Glad to see you.

(160)

Happy, sad, and disappointing memories of your loved one are stored in your mind. Your loved one may have hurt you and you still feel hurt. Though you cannot forget this memory, you can forgive.

(161)

Beauty can be hidden or unnoticed. Shadows can be intriguing. Rain trickling down a windowpane can be beautiful. Feast your eyes on hidden aspects of beauty, for they are everywhere.

(162)

When your loved one died you may have inherited their pet. The pet is a connection to your loved one, and you take good care of it. Caring for the pet helps you care for you.

(163)

Some believe in signs from their loved ones—a cardinal, hawk, or butterfly. You watch for these signs and tell yourself your loved one is not gone. They are in another realm.

(164)

Your grief differs greatly from a friend's grief. This happens because you are at different stages of grief and have different experiences with it. Still, you are on a shared journey and may take it together.

(165)

According to a folk song, grief came knocking at the door. You asked, "What shall I do?" You ask this question many times. Do what you need to do. Live the best life you can in memory of your loved one.

(166)

Suffering is not the best teacher. Love, kindness, and patience are better ones. Take mental notes. Learn from these experiences. You always were a quick learner.

(167)

Look around and you will find something good. The airline may let you fly home for free. Your loved one may have pre-arranged for burial. Goodness helps you get through grief. Because of goodness you have hope.

(168)

There will be days that do not make sense. Everything is "off." Rather than fighting these days, save your energy and go with the flow. Normal days will return. Savor each one.

(169)

Optimism, like leadership, can be learned. Reprogram your mind by keeping a gratitude journal. Every so often, read an excerpt from your journal aloud—so many experiences, so much gratitude.

(170)

When you live with someone a long time, they become part of your soul. Your loved one's personality, talents, and accomplishments affect your identity. These memories are companions for your grief journey.

(171)

Do not let the loneliness of grief leach joy from your life. Think about all the enjoyable activities you can do alone. Make a list of them. Try several things on the list. You are in good company.

(172)

Your loved one may appear in a dream. The dream is like watching a movie with a plot, colors, and conversation. Keeping a dream journal may help you. Write about your dream as soon as you wake up or you will forget it.

(173)

Go inward. Meditate regularly and spend time with yourself. Choose a word to think about, such as *father*. Continue to meditate about *father* and all its meanings. You could meditate about this word for weeks.

(174)

The death of a sibling changes life forever. You lost your companion, best friend, confidant, and cheerleader. Instead of caring for yourself, you may care for your parents. Start taking care of you.

(175)

Having an attitude of gratitude changes grief. Continue to keep your gratitude journal and make regular entries. Be grateful for these thoughts. Now and then, read a page from your journal aloud.

(176)

Just when you were doing well, you suddenly feel terrible. Give yourself a healing tune-up. Eat right, get enough sleep, and count your blessings. Your grief is slowly healing. Be glad.

(177)

Quiet help can be strong help. Seek out a quiet friend who has grief experience. Have coffee with them and share snippets of your lives. Let your friend's strength strengthen you.

(178)

You made it through the day without crying. Today was better than yesterday. Tomorrow will be better than today. Your loved one is part of every moment of life.

(179)

Grief is confusing. Others may see you more clearly than you see yourself. Consult a relative or friend about your healing. How do they think you are doing? Think about what they say.

(180)

Prayer enables you to look inside yourself, assess things, and ask for help. Say a prayer now if you believe in the power of prayer. Pray for others while you are praying for yourself.

(181)

You cannot change facts but can change your response to them. Though you are devastated by grief, be grateful for your loved one's life. Draw upon this love in the years to come.

(182)

You have moments when you feel sorry for yourself. This is a normal response to grief. Instead of feeling sorry, which is a waste of time, be grateful for what you have now.

(183)

Repetitive thoughts in your journal are proof of their importance. You are still thinking about these ideas. Pay attention to these topics. Your subconscious mind is telling you something.

(184)

Be thankful for the people who helped your loved one: doctors, nurses, hospice staff, clergy, relatives, neighbors, and volunteers. Life is not a solitary journey. Neither is death.

(185)

Make alone times creative times. Finish a project, start a new one, express yourself with gardening, reorganize the pantry, whatever. Creative times help ease your grief.

(186)

Healing grief takes resolve and practice. Both are equally important, but resolve comes first. Be determined. Grief healing is within your reach.

(187)

You think of your loved one every day. Tell them you love them. Say it aloud and mean it. Listen to your voice as you say these words.

(188)

The death of a loved one is not punishment for something you did. Delete this idea from your mind. Death is part of the life cycle and part of the universe. Let your star shine brightly.

(189)

You need to feel grounded. What does the foundation of your life include? Draw two parallel lines on paper. Add circular stones in the middle big enough for words. Write something that grounds you on each stone.

(190)

Bitterness comes from hurt. This corrosive emotion eats away at you. Bypass feelings of bitterness. Replace them with feelings of kindness and caring. You will be better for them.

(191)

Friends can be honest with each other. A dear friend may keep giving you advice. You appreciate their advice but do not need to follow it. Thank your friend and say you are advising yourself.

(192)

Lists can help you solve problems. Make a list of the things you miss after your loved one died. Life is different without these things. Can you replace any of the things on your list with action?

(193)

You need to honor all types of grief to understand it. Grief includes having a miscarriage, being passed over for promotion, losing a job, death of a beloved pet, and the end of a relationship. Show compassion for friends and yourself.

(194)

You can have positive thoughts even though you are grieving. Write a positive thought on paper. Stick the paper in your pocket. Make this your thought of the day. Take it out and read it when you are sad.

(195)

Enjoy one of life's simple pleasures. Sit on a park bench and feel the warmth of the sun. Listen to birds sing. Smell the freshly mowed grass. Watch the people who pass by. Be glad you are alive.

(196)

Promote grief healing by taking care of your physical self. Try to eat a balanced diet, get regular physical activity, and turn off your cell phone one hour before bedtime. You will sleep better.

(197)

Talk with those who have experienced grief. What feeling was hardest for them? For you? Discuss the ways of coping that worked best. Be courageous and try one.

(198)

Grief can make your body tense. Relax with body meditation. Sit in a comfortable chair. Close your eyes. Starting with your head, slowly relax your neck, arms, chest, tummy, legs, and feet. Become as limp as a rag doll.

(199)

Grief has aftershocks. Your feelings subside and, like unplanted farmland, lie fallow for a while. Are you back to square one? Not really. Dust off your coping skills and use them.

(200)

Just one more, you plead, one more conversation with your loved one. You will never have that conversation. Find strength in the happy conversations you had in the past. Make these conversations part of the present.

(201)

You never said goodbye to your loved one and feel terrible about it. This fact cannot be changed. Write a goodbye letter to your loved one. Put it in a drawer. There, you have said goodbye.

(202)

Walk in the woods to soothe your soul. Notice the height of the trees, the texture of the bark, and the shape of the leaves. Trees reach upward toward the light. May you reach upward like the trees.

A NEW AND MEANINGFUL LIFE

(203)

Continue to walk your healing path and see where it leads. Though the way is dark, stay on the path. Take one forward step today and another one tomorrow. Keep walking to the future.

(204)

The thought is as loud as a thunderclap: "I am my loved one's legacy." Think about what your legacy could be. What might it include? Choose a legacy that would make your loved one—and you—proud.

(205)

Grief makes you feel like life is out of control. If you think about it, however, you realize you still control some things. Brainstorm on the control you have. Take action to regain some control. You are in charge of you.

(206)

When you start to visualize the future, you are moving beyond survival mode. You survived the death of your loved one. Now it is time to thrive and kick up your heels. Continue to plan your future and add details. Your future is shaping up nicely.

(207)

You have been home so long you feel like you are living in a cocoon. Maybe it is time to venture out of the safety and security of your home. Peek outside and look around. Get outside today.

(208)

Log in to the internet. Choose a book you think a grieving friend might enjoy. Arrange for the book to be sent to them along with a note that reads, "Sending heartfelt condolences. This book comes with virtual hugs."

(209)

Grief was part of your old life and will be part of your new life. Make peace with the fact that grief has no closure. Yet grief has made you a stronger person. Build on this strength.

(210)

You cannot remember your loved one's face clearly. How upsetting! Do not despair. When this happens, study a photo of your loved one. See the love on their face and feel that love.

(211)

Believe in yourself and in tomorrow. Though you will have some missteps, you may correct them and learn from them. You can learn a lot from missteps. Happiness is just around the corner.

(212)

Be honest with your feelings. According to grief experts, grief needs to be witnessed so healing can take place. Family members and dear friends can be your witnesses. You may be your own witness too.

(213)

Start a one-word journal. Think of a word that describes your day and write it in a notepad. This word may be *lost* or *improving* or *hopeful*. Each word is a stepping-stone to your new life.

(214)

Harrowing as it is, grief does not define you. Grief makes you a new, improved version of yourself. Make this vow: *I choose to grow from grief.* Take action on this vow.

(215)

Send email messages to the people who sent you cards. Two sentences will do it. Say you are grateful for the sender's kindness. You may be so grateful you burst into tears.

(216)

Grief is a journey of self-discovery. Along the way you learn surprising things. You wish you could have learned these things differently, but that did not happen. Look grief in the face and hold your ground. Grief begone!

(217)

Alone times help you get to know yourself. You may realize that you are impatient, for example. Make the most from your alone times and learn from them. You are in good company.

(218)

Your loved one does not need to be present for you to have a relationship with them. Memories and experiences still connect you with your loved one. Be aware of this relationship and how it changes you.

(219)

Continue to practice the art of self-healing. You have made significant progress and, as you get to know the new you, continue to make progress. Give yourself a pat on the back for effort.

(220)

Sorrowful feelings are always with you. The length of your grief hinges on how long your loved one was ill and the cause of death. Keep working on acceptance. The death of your loved one influences how you will live.

(221)

Singing brings people together in community. Maybe that is why traveling sing-alongs are so popular. Join a singing group if it comes to your town. Sing with all your heart.

(222)

What is real life? It is what you are experiencing this moment. Though you still feel caught between sorrow and hope, you are alive. You are here and that is a blessing.

(223)

Watch for signs of hope: fewer tears, smiling more often, laughing aloud, a positive attitude, acting more alert, better observation skills, and believing in the future. All contribute to healing.

(224)

Prepare for avoidance if you are a bereaved parent. The death of a child is the worst thing that can happen to any parent. People may shy away from you. This is not a personal response: it is situational.

(225)

Caregiving is love in action. You know this if you were your loved one's caregiver. Thank you for getting up early, working late, continuing to learn, and tackling messy jobs. Your care prolonged your loved one's life. Be proud of that.

(226)

In the spring, florists, nurseries, discount stores, and grocery stores stock up on plants. The variety of plants is impressive. Buy a pot of daisies if you see them. You deserve a day brightener.

(227)

Picasso said people who saw beauty in humble places were blessed. Check humble places in your neighborhood for beauty. You may be surprised at all the beauty you discover.

(228)

Today, photos are stored in the cloud. (I expect to look at clouds and see words I wrote.) Store your photos in an album instead. Looking at photos brings back happy memories. Be grateful for them.

(229)

Make a list of your loved one's values. Read the list on the anniversary of their death. Give copies of the list to relatives and friends. Make their values your values. Pass them on to the next generation.

(230)

Enlarge a photo of your loved one or have it enlarged. The photo may also be transferred to canvas. Looking at the photo helps you feel your loved one's presence and contributes to a sense of peace.

(231)

Your loved one had a favorite color and wore it often. Wear this color in memory of them. Like a ribbon, this color ties you and your loved one together. What color is your ribbon?

(232)

Recall your loved one's expressions. Imitate their humor. Try one of their hobbies. Doing these things makes you feel like your loved one is alive. And in a way, they are.

(233)

Nature is healing. Walk outdoors today. Look for birds, budding flowers, playing children, and beautiful architecture. There is so much to see. Make these sights part of your soul.

(234)

What is your purpose now? Your life purpose may be the same or different. Maybe your purpose is a total surprise. Whatever your purpose is, make the most of it. Keep working on your purpose.

(235)

The death of a spouse or partner reduces your income. Before you spend money, ask yourself, "Do I *need* this, or do I *want* it?" You may not be a math whiz, but you understand cash flow and can manage finances.

(236)

A vision board is a planning tool. Cut out magazine pictures of what you want your new life to be. A different town. An apartment instead of a house. Tennis lessons. Paste the pictures on cardboard. Now work on turning vision board dreams into reality.

(237)

Are you on a journey of grief reconciliation or recovery? The answer may be neither. You are on a healing journey, a worthy goal. Approach it in stages.

(238)

Try a walking meditation. Walk a few steps. Stop, breathe, and observe your surroundings. Repeat this pattern and become more observant with each step. You live in a wonderful world.

(239)

Unacknowledged losses are losses others fail to see. These losses are like thorns that prick you again and again. Unacknowledged losses affect your body, mind, and spirit. Track these losses because they are powerful.

(240)

You start reading books again. Because you are grieving, you peek at the endings first. (Somewhere in my literary travels, I learned this is immature.) Add your name—and mine—to the immature list. Read the ending if you want to.

(241)

While your loved one was dying, you may have ignored your own health. You wind up in the hospital emergency room and start crying. This is understandable. Your loved one is with you in spirit. Focus on this thought.

(242)

You continue to read about grief. Reading helps you understand its symptoms, responses, and challenges. This is not a solitary journey. Books are your friends, a font of information and comfort.

(243)

Your loved one should be with you, drinking coffee or tea, reading a magazine, and talking about the news. There will always be a gaping hole in your life. Make peace with this and keep your eyes on the future.

(244)

Just because you've always washed sheets on Mondays does not mean you always need to do it. Unless you tromped through mud, sheets can wait. This is a time to be kind to yourself. You have more interesting things to do than laundry.

(245)

Adult coloring books are the rage, so popular that coloring clubs have sprung up coast to coast. These books are available in a variety of topics: healing, relaxation, mindfulness, or grief. Buy a book and start coloring.

(246)

New grief sparks old grief. You feel like your grief has doubled. There is no shortcut to grief. Say these words: "I survived grief before and will survive it again."

(247)

Enso means "circle" in Japanese and painting them is relaxing. Get some plain paper, black paint, and brushes of different widths. To paint an enso, meditate for a minute or two, take a deep breath, and make a circle with one brush stroke. Each circle is unique, just like you.

(248)

You cannot stay in contact with all your friends but can stay in contact with some. Email or call a friend today. They will be glad to hear from you. Share your news and listen to theirs. One friend can lead you through the darkness.

(249)

Make this a surprise day. Do something you did not plan to do. Walk to the public library. Get lunch from a food truck. Order the shirt you wanted for weeks. Surprise days are fun.

(250)

Though you are grieving, you have blessings in your life. Blessings are more meaningful when they are shared. The ability to share a blessing is a blessing itself. What blessing could you share today?

(251)

You can still learn while you are grieving. Take a writing course. Express your feelings in affirmations, a story, memoir, or guide. Share your writing with family members.

(252)

Set a framed photo of your loved one by their place at the table. While you are eating with family, share stories of your loved one. Decide which story is the favorite of the day.

(253)

In the past few months, you may not have been the friend you wanted to be. Grief distracted you, and you feel badly about this. Give your friends some credit. They know you are grieving and understand.

(254)

Your loved one may have had sayings—one-sentence words of advice. These sayings are part of your conversation. Add another saying to your collection: *I will survive grief and thrive.* Make this your mission.

(255)

Trees symbolize life. Plant a tree in the yard in memory of your loved one. When you do this, you honor them and help the environment. What kind of tree will you choose?

(256)

You started journaling but, along the way, the entries waned. Resume journal writing today. Write about your experiences, feelings, and challenges. Consult your journal as you plan your future.

(257)

Start a doodling journal. Buy a sketchbook and doodle about grief. Your doodles do not have to be perfect, but they do need to represent you. When the sketchbook is full, buy another. Continue to doodle your way through grief.

(258)

Ask a friend how they coped with grief. Can their ideas help you? Pick an idea and start working on it today.

(259)

Special days trigger grief. You may burst into tears on your loved one's birthday or Christmas. Prepare for grief triggers. Do something different, hang out with friends, or take a weekend trip.

(260)

Grief and guilt. What a combination! In fact, guilt prolongs grief—something you do not need right now. Worrying about guilt eats away at you. Say goodbye to guilt.

(261)

The word *legacy* usually refers to the past. *Legacy* also refers to the present. What is your legacy? You may choose resilience. (It is what I chose.) Model resilience for your grandchildren. Show them you have faith in life and yourself.

(262)

Grief is an uncertain time. As time passes you learn to live with uncertainty. This hard-earned skill makes you stronger and girds you for the future.

(263)

Every time you try a new way of coping, surprise yourself, or practice self-care, you are building resilience. Step by step, you add to the core of strength within you.

(264)

Become a grief detective. What boulders block your happiness? Identify them and push the boulders aside with action and more action. Claim happiness for yourself. You deserve it.

(265)

Living without a loved one takes courage. You need this courage at the start of your grief journey and beyond. Each day, you renew your courage and find that courage in love.

(266)

Each of us has the power to make a new and meaningful life. (I am working on continuing to be creative.) Pick a topic that interests you and set goals to go with it. Start working on a goal and see what happens.

(267)

Despite the progress you have made, you still feel stressed. While you were not looking your stress became chronic. De-stress with physical activities, mindfulness, and meditation. Make these coping strategies part of every day.

(268)

Diet influences recovery. You may be eating snack food "meals." Whether it is breakfast, lunch, or dinner, try to eat a balanced diet. Take a multivitamin if you are not eating four to five plant-based foods a day.

(269)

Your feelings bounce around like a rubber ball. Grief mood swings are normal. As time passes, you begin to see hope and your moods even out. Hope keeps you going.

(270)

Hire an experienced sewer to make a quilt from your loved one's clothing or, if you can, make it yourself. Choose a classic pattern—squares, stars, or leaves. Sleep under the quilt at bedtime and remember your loved one.

(271)

What is on the schedule? Look through the mail as you usually do. Find a walking buddy. Talk to your neighbor. These are ordinary things in an extraordinary day. You are alive and breathing.

(272)

Always is often an overused word. When it comes to love, *always* may be an underused word. You will always feel your beloved's love. Find strength in this. Let love be your compass and your guide.

(273)

Contrary to what some believe, grief is not depression. Grief is a normal response to a tragic event. You are coping and changing and learning. That is all a human being can do.

(274)

Continue to doodle your way through grief. Disappointments can be blessings in disguise. Make a list of your blessings.

(275)

Create the happiness you seek. Build on your strengths, talents, goals, positivity, and the new memories you create. Claim happiness for yourself.

(276)

Give your new life new meaning. Try a different tack and see how it works out. Change course if you feel you are headed in the wrong direction.

(277)

Say this sentence this morning and every morning: *Love is stronger than death.* You still love your loved one and always will. Love will lead you forward.

MAKING GOOD
FROM GRIEF

(278)

Looking forward to the future is not a betrayal of your loved one. On the contrary, it is tribute to them. Happiness comes from inside you. Put as much effort into creating a happy future as you put into grief healing.

(279)

You stand at the threshold of the unknown, one of the most difficult thresholds of life. Believe in yourself. Believe in experience. Believe in the future and welcome it with outstretched arms.

(280)

Make peace with the residual pain of grief. You have come this far and can go further. Stay on your healing path. Your progress is steady, and your resolve is strong.

(281)

Brainstorm ways of giving to others. Instead of giving money, give a friend the moral support they need. Serve on a committee. Volunteer for community project. Time is one of the most valuable gifts you can give.

(282)

You have changed. Hope has returned and you feel it in your soul. Earlier in your grief journey, you needed moral support. Now you are standing on your own. Cheer for yourself.

(283)

Talk about grief brain with other bereaved people. Many have never heard the term and will be glad to know about it. Compare signs of grief brain and coping strategies. Everyone benefits from this discussion.

(284)

After all the sorrow, you need a change of pace. Join an organization, club, or group. Attend meetings regularly and try to get to know the members. Making new friends adds zest to your life.

(285)

Create a memory tree. Stick a bare branch in a pot of dirt. Cut leaf shapes from colored paper. Write memories of your loved one on the leaves. Hang the leaves on the tree with string or tape them. Continue to add leaves to the tree.

(286)

Add a new chapter to your family history. Encourage children to think about leadership and model good leadership for them. Grief needs good leaders too. Be one.

(287)

Send a thank you note or card to the hospital or hospice floor. Be specific about how the staff helped when you needed help. Do not send flowers or balloons because they will not be accepted.

(288)

Grief expert Judy Tatelbaum thinks bereaved people can choose to be creative survivors. The creative survivor role leads to endless possibilities. Explore them with fervor.

(289)

Continue to improve your grief literacy. Read books about grief, symptoms, coping, and healing. Share the books with bereaved friends. You may wish to create your own mini library of references.

(290)

You have developed wisdom on your grief journey. Be aware of this newfound wisdom. Share it when you are asked or feel it is appropriate.

(291)

Active listening requires more energy than passive listening. Become an active listener. Show you are listening by nodding your head. This day, give some-one the gift of listening.

(292)

Remind the world that your loved one lived. Post on social media if you are comfortable doing this. Continue to tell stories about your loved one. Feel a linking object that comforts you.

(293)

Place a pot of flowers on your loved one's grave. Talk to your loved one while you are there. Water the plant when the soil becomes dry. You tended to your loved one in life and tend to them in death.

(294)

Some establish nonprofit organizations in memory of their loved one. Consider this idea. If the idea is intimidating, volunteer for an established nonprofit organization. Help is always needed.

(295)

You may have tested positive for Covid-19 and have been quarantined. Since you cannot leave your home, you order groceries online. You miss shopping for yourself and seeing friends. Find other ways to socialize.

(296)

Mother's Day and Father's Day are tough holidays. Do something in memory of your child. Donate art supplies to a nursery school, sports equipment to a high school, or books to a library. Honor your child with action.

(297)

A few words can bolster family members, friends, and colleagues. Give them honest, one-sentence compliments. People will remember the compliments and so will you.

(298)

Start a new ritual in memory of your loved one. You may plant tulip bulbs each spring, for example. Share the ritual with family members and friends. Invite them to participate next spring.

(299)

The words *happiness* and *joy* are used interchangeably, yet they have different meanings. Happiness is external—a feeling based on other people, places, and events. Joy is internal and comes from your soul. Be open to joy.

(300)

Make a memory book about your loved one. Include photos, receipts, theater programs, and newspaper articles—anything that represents your loved one's life. More information about memory books is available online.

(301)

Do random acts of kindness in memory of your loved one. Try to do several acts each month. You are continuing your loved one's generosity. Random acts of kindness help you more than those who receive them.

(302)

Accepting the death of a child is a lifelong process. Spend time with other bereaved parents. You have so much in common. A weekend retreat can be a salve for your wounds.

(303)

Your loved one's bedroom is like a hospital room. When you look at all the stuff—the hospital bed, over-the-bed table, standing frame, wheelchair, and shower wheelchair—you sob. Give these things away. Make the room a happy room again.

(304)

Think of your loved one's outstanding traits and make it part of your life. (I call these connections Action Memorials.) Get a birdfeeder if your loved one was a birdwatcher. Serve on a committee in memory of your loved one. Action Memorials connect you with your loved one every day.

(305)

Give a bereaved person the gift of listening. Ask them about their loved one. Listen attentively. Show you are listening by giving one-word answers. End the conversation with, "Thank you for sharing your memories."

(306)

Attend a lecture or workshop about writing your obituary. Who knew so much was involved? If you cannot find a talk or workshop on the topic, contact the director of a community education program and suggest it.

(307)

Some resort to emotional spending to cope with grief. Avoid this trap. Go on a giving spree instead. Give your loved one's clothes to charity or gently used books to the library.

(308)

Making memory teddy bears from a deceased loved one's clothes is a trend. Order a teddy bear from the manufacturer or make it from a free pattern you download. Give the teddy bear to your grandchild or yourself.

(309)

Several years down the grief road, offer to be a buddy for a grieving friend. Call them regularly. Send cards regularly. Let your friend know you are there for them.

(310)

Golf clubs are pushed to the back of the closet. Craft supplies are gathering dust. You do not have time for hobbies and feel doubly bereft. Resume one of your hobbies. Having a hobby makes you feel whole again.

(311)

If you were married to your loved one for many years, you know their values. You lived these values. Pick one value and focus on it. Pass this value on to your grandkids.

(312)

Give linking objects to your grandkids. A grand-daughter may receive your loved one's clock. A grandson may receive your loved one's tools. (I gave my husband's medical bag to my physician grand-son.) Linking objects are reminders of love.

(313)

Donate hymnals to your church. Check with the publisher about unit cost and bulk rates. Before the hymnals are dispersed, put memory bookplates inside the front covers.

(314)

Your kindness continues your loved one's kindness. Honor your loved one with an act of kindness today. What will it be? Why did you choose it?

(315)

"New normal" is a common term. People use it to describe changes in their lives. Unfortunately, you may not find a new normal. Do not waste time worrying about this. You are alive and that is what counts.

(316)

Assess your grief healing. How are you different now? Make a list of your accomplishments. You have come a long way.

(317)

Nobody recovers completely from grief. You will always feel a sense of loss. When you are stronger, offer to help someone who is grieving. Provide taxi service, deliver takeout, or grocery shop for them. Helping them helps you.

(318)

Join a church prayer group. Pray for all who grieve—relatives, church members, friends, parents, siblings, children, grandchildren, grandparents, health care workers, police, and military families. Pray with all your heart.

(319)

Participate in a webinar about growing from grief. Enter questions if you have them. You never know what you will learn.

(320)

Learning to live without a loved one is a challenge. You review your life—things you didn't do and things you did. Poet John O'Donohue would describe this process as coming home to yourself. You may not know it yet, but you can be true to yourself and enjoy the miracle of life.

(321)

Write a poem about your loved one. Start with the words "I remember" and see where the idea leads you. Share your poem with family members. They may want to write their own poems.

(322)

Surprising as it sounds, giving helps heal your grief. Send sympathy cards to bereaved friends. Stay active in your religious/spiritual community. When you give to others, they give back to you.

(323)

Ask the park commission if you can plant some flowers in the park in memory of your loved one. If your request is approved, plant flowers and add a memorial sign if possible.

(324)

"Mindfulness" is a popular word. What does it mean? This word refers to acute awareness of your feelings, body, and mind. This is your day. Make it a mindful one.

(325)

Help remove the taboo of talking about death by bringing up the topic. Talk about your loved one, how you coped, and how you are healing. This takes courage but you are helping other bereaved people and the community.

(326)

With help from family members, donate to a college scholarship fund. The college may have matching funds that increase the amount of the scholarship. You will help a dedicated student.

(327)

After a loved one dies your thoughts fall into a pattern of remembering, reflection, and renewal. The intensity of your feelings is not the only thing that changes. You renew yourself each day.

(328)

Find out if other bereaved people are using adult coloring books. Gather four or five together and form a coloring book club. Meet at your home, if possible, and serve light refreshments.

(309)

Work with a school librarian to create a section of grief books for children. Contribute to the cost of the books if possible. Arrange for a comfortable reading chair to be placed near the books.

(330)

Approach the day with gladness and you will have a good day. (I think of my mother's words, "I lived my life at the best time. I went to school in a horse-drawn carriage and saw men walk on the moon.") This is a good day to have a good day.

(331)

The US Forestry Service and other organizations plant trees in memory of the deceased. Trees are planted in national forests damaged by fire. Pay for a grove of trees to be planted in memory of your loved one. What a touching memorial.

(332)

Think about your values. Choose the one that is most important to you. Do something to support this value. You will always be a work in progress.

(333)

Review grief books for an organization's newsletter or your church newsletter. Cite the features of the book and why it helped you. Use the five-star rating system if you can.

(334)

Your loved one accumulated dozens of books. What can you do with them? Give books to relatives, the public library, or Little Library in your neighborhood. Books change lives and you are doing that.

(335)

Partner with your religious community to commission a song in memory of your loved one. (A composer friend may be willing to write a song for free.) Share the song with the choir. Invite family members and friends to the premier of the song.

(336)

Treasure the laughs you shared with your loved one. Listen carefully and you may still hear their laughter. Laugh as often as you can. Catch laughs as they go by.

(337)

Before your loved one died, you talked with them about who would get what. Now you are distributing their things. Carrying out your loved one's wishes is an act of love that tugs at your heartstrings.

(338)

Donate equipment or supplies to a high school, junior college, college or university, or trade school in memory of your loved one. This is a fitting memorial, one that continues your loved one's interests.

(339)

Join a grief book discussion group. If a group is not available, form your own. Find a meeting place that is convenient for everyone. Are you going to meet once a week, biweekly or once a month?

(340)

Just as each person's grief is unique, your healing path is unique. As your journey progresses, you see light ahead. That shaft of light is hope.

(341)

If you are the oldest family member, the death of a loved one makes you leader of the pack. You are now the matriarch, patriarch, or group leader. Accept this role gladly. The family needs you and that may be why you lived so long.

(342)

Telling stories about your loved one keeps them alive in your mind. You may have a favorite story and keep telling it. Do not worry about being repetitious. The joy on your face brings joy to others.

(343)

What part of grief healing was hardest for you? Create an hour-long talk about it. Submit your talk to a conference committee. Give your talk on Zoom.

(344)

In the computer age, everyone is an author. Write a book about your grief. You can do it! Avoid the first line, "It was a dark and stormy night." That line has been used already.

(345)

If you have not done this yet, look at the public library's grief books for kids. Update and add to the collection if you can. Make sure there is a sign that identifies the collection. Donate a book yearly in memory of your loved one.

(346)

You were always compassionate. Grief made you more so. What can you give to others? Give them your time, flowers from the garden, or homemade banana bread. Thank you for giving.

(347)

Looking for a support group? Start your own. Select a meeting place and set the hours. Establish ground rules and read them at every meeting. The most important rule: *What is said in group stays in group.*

(348)

Continue to say, "I love you." Say it to family members, grandkids, and friends. Life is short. This may be your last chance to express the love you feel.

(349)

Make a gift for a grieving friend. Get a medium-size jar with a lid. Write Bible quotations on small pieces of paper or quotations from other religious texts. Put the papers in the jar. Tie a bow around the top with a tag that says, "Rx for grief healing. Read a quote a day."

(350)

Mail a packet of seeds to a grieving friend. Enclose a "Thinking of you" card with a note that says, "Let the love you felt for _____ continue to grow like these seeds."

(351)

Volunteer in memory of your loved one. Your options include volunteering at the public library, local hospital, nursing home, food bank, or your religious community. Volunteering reconnects you with the world.

(352)

Deliver a meal to a grieving friend. Before you pre-pare the meal, call ahead and see if food would be appreciated. Too much food results in spoiled food, which makes the recipient feel badly.

(353)

Step outside your comfort zone. Prepare a talk about the healing step that helped you most. Give the talk to a support group or a religious group.

(354)

Do not let your loved one's treasures gather dust. Give their collection (artwork, wood tools, etc.) to the art museum or historical society. Your loved one would be pleased.

(355)

Compile a cookbook of your loved one's favorite recipes/foods. Type the recipes and put them in plastic page protectors. Insert the pages in a three-ring binder. (I did this after my mother-in-law died. *Favorite Recipes from Nana's Recipe Box* was a holiday hit.) Remember to make a cookbook for yourself.

(356)

Start a support group for widows or widowers. Ask others to join. Make the get-togethers casual and thoughtful. There is an abundance of wisdom in this group.

(357)

Bereaved people help one another. Call a grieving friend, leave flowers on the doorstep, or deliver chicken soup. Grief is easier to bear when it is shared.

(358)

Your loved one's life was a book. Research online publishing companies. Find one you can afford. Publish a book about your loved one. Give copies to family members.

(359)

Make a caring basket for a grieving friend. Put tissue paper on the bottom of the basket. Fill it with a blank journal, a pen, cookies, tea bags, tissues, and a note that says, "So sorry for your loss. Thinking of you."

(360)

You remember your loved one and, when you die, hope others remember you. Volunteer at the local food bank, read to nursing home residents, start a container garden. Do something memorable today.

(361)

Make a joy timeline. Draw a horizontal line in the middle of a piece of paper. Note joyful times above the line. Note the dates below the line. You had joyful experiences in the past and will experience joy again.

(362)

The death of your loved one has added new meaning to your life. Compare old meanings with new ones. You may have felt like a victim, for example, and chose to be a survivor.

(363)

Assemble personal care packs—comb, shampoo, toothbrush, toothpaste, deodorant, and emery boards —in plastic zipper bags. Donate the personal care packs to the homeless in memory of your loved one.

(364)

Making meaning is the last stage of grief, according to grief expert David Kessler. You may agree with him. Searching for meaning takes time. As months pass, your meaning becomes clearer. Blessings to you.

(*365*)

Gather your healing bouquet together—your sorrows, memories, feelings, experiences, talents, hopes, and dreams. Hold the bouquet with clasped hands. Live each day of your life like a prayer.

ABOUT THE AUTHOR

Harriet Hodgson has been a freelancer for forty-four years and is the author of thousands of articles and forty-four books. She has a BS in Early Childhood Education from Wheelock College of Education and Human Development, an MA in Art Education from the University of Minnesota, and additional graduate training. Hodgson is Assistant Editor of the Open to Hope website, www.opentohope.com.

She is a member of the Association of Health Care Journalists, Alliance of Independent Authors, Minnesota Coalition for Death Education and Support, and Grief Coalition of Southeastern Minnesota.

Hodgson has appeared on more than 190 talk shows, dozens of BlogTalkRadio shows and television stations, including CNN. A popular speaker, she has given presentations at public health, Alzheimer's, caregiving, and bereavement conferences. The award-winning author lives in Rochester, Minnesota. Visit www.harriethodgson.com to learn more about this grandmother, great-grandmother, community volunteer, author, and speaker.

GRIEF RESOURCES BY HARRIET HODGSON

Grief Doodling: Bringing Back Your Smiles

From Sad to Glad
(workbook for kids ages 5-8)

From Darkness to Sunshine
(workbook for kids ages 9-12)

Writing to Recover Journal

*Happy Again: Your New and Meaningful Life
After Loss*

*101 Affirmations to Ease Your Grief Journey:
Words of Comfort, Words of Hope*

*Seed Time: Growing from Life's Disappointments,
Losses, and Sorrows*

Smiling Through Your Tears: Anticipating Grief,
Lois Krahn, MD, co-author

ANOTHER WRITELIFE GRIEF BOOK BY HARRIET HODGSON

Grief Doodling is a different approach to coping with loss. It gets tweens and teens to participate, think, set goals, and start walking a healing path.

From the very first page, *Grief Doodling* invites action. Topics range from the benefits of doodling, to why doodling is fun, to doodling tips, and responding to doodling prompts. The prompts, based on grief research, promote self-worth and healing.

"This is a hopeful book—something all grieving kids need. *Grief Doodling* will take the reader's hand and lead them down an inspiring and whimsical path toward healing. Hodgson has created a magnificent tool that every person experiencing loss should have at their fingertips. I love this book!"

— Sandy Goodman, grief speaker and author of *Love Never Dies*